Medieval Meets Baroque Illuminated Calligraphy Alphabet with Rhymes

Fine Art of Hand Lettering

Valerie Rachel Martin

Copyright © 2020 Valerie Rachel Martin
All rights reserved.
ISBN: **9798662966222**

About this book

I am an artist of many interests and many projects, and even more-than-many shelved projects "until I have more time" kind. This illuminated alphabet started as illustrations of my novel *Veronica Larose*. The young protagonist travels the world in search of magic. This is why all the letters represent something she would consider magical. Then, as many a self-doubting artist or author, I changed my mind and forgot about my magical letters, until the pandemic of 2020. With so much time on my hands, I blew the dust off the sketchbook and redid the entire alphabet from scratch.

In addition to illustrations, I came up with lighthearted rhymes to accompany each letter. Then I made my project even more challenging, and wrote out the rhymes in a variety of calligraphy styles: Chancery, Uncial, Copperplate Script, and Old English Gothic.

Calligraphy and the art of hand lettering have been my passion since the early days of art school. Thanks to the old-school profs who insisted we, the young wild things, learn this dying art. We are talking early 80's. Consider calligraphy was a dying art back then. What about now, in 2020 something? I am glad to know of a small and dedicated following of scribes still exists and keeps this art form alive.

Art is never static - it evolves. So does calligraphy. More than millennia later, calligraphy has adapted from the old writing tradition into new styles, with modern or traditional writing instruments and inks.

In the postmodern era, we have no boundaries on how to stretch and fuse artistic concepts. In this Illuminated Alphabet book, Gothic and Baroque lettering styles create a delightful fusion. Medieval style illumination with illustrations of magical and mythical creatures makes letters come alive. Hand-written witty rhymes show examples of calligraphy hands.

The purpose of this book is to provide fun and inspiration to readers of any age. Perhaps this would be their first step towards learning the art of fine hand lettering.

Hands used in this book

Calligraphy styles from centuries ago are called *Hands*, or later - *typefaces*. In modern language, *typefaces* are sometimes called *fonts*.

However, *fonts* exist as computer applications. *Hands* are always handwritten or illustrated by a calligrapher or artist.

Uncial is an ancient book Hand characterized by rounded strokes and no capitalization. It originated in the 2nd-century AD.

Old English Gothic is also known as Black Letter, or Gothic. This style of writing was prevalent throughout Western Europe from the early 12th until the 17th century.

Chancery Black encompasses two styles of calligraphy, a written form of Black Letter from France and England in the 13th century, presented in this book. In the early 15th century, Chancery Hand traveled to Italy became italic cursive handwriting.

Copperplate Script is a style of calligraphic writing done with a pointed dip pen. It dates from the early 18th century when a quill was a primary writing instrument. Copperplate Script is also a general term for various forms of scripts that evolved from the traditional English Roundhead.

Uncial
Old English Gothic
Chancery Black
Copperplate Script

Garamond is the typeface used in this book.

Garamond is a serif typeface named for 16th-century Parisian engraver Claude Garamond. Garamond-style typefaces were popular because they resemble elegant old style calligraphy, and often used for book printing.

Angel

The hope is here

When an angel is near

And sadness disappears

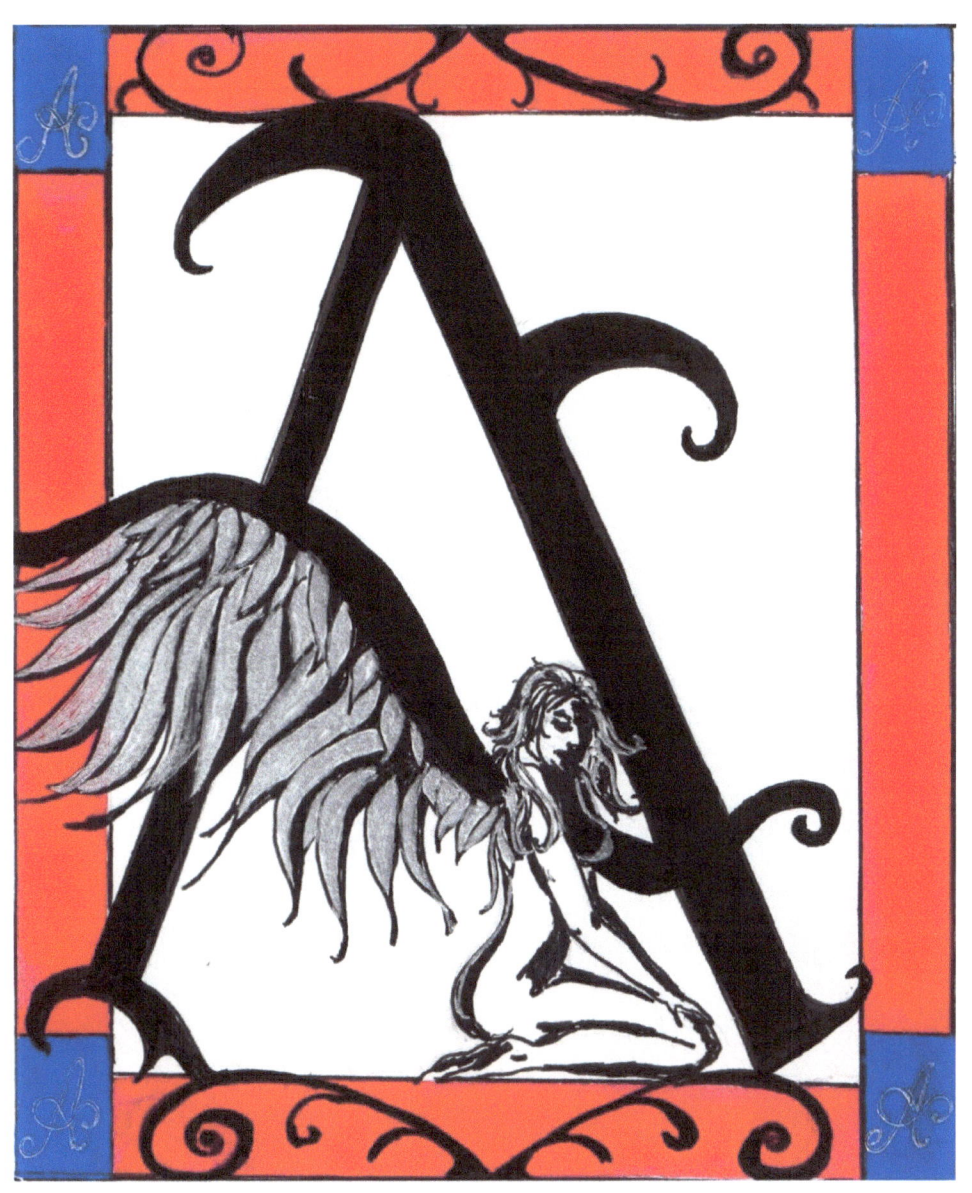

The hope is here
When an angel is near
And sadness disappears

Bacchus

Fun and wine

With frolic divine

Come drink and dance

While you still

Have a chance

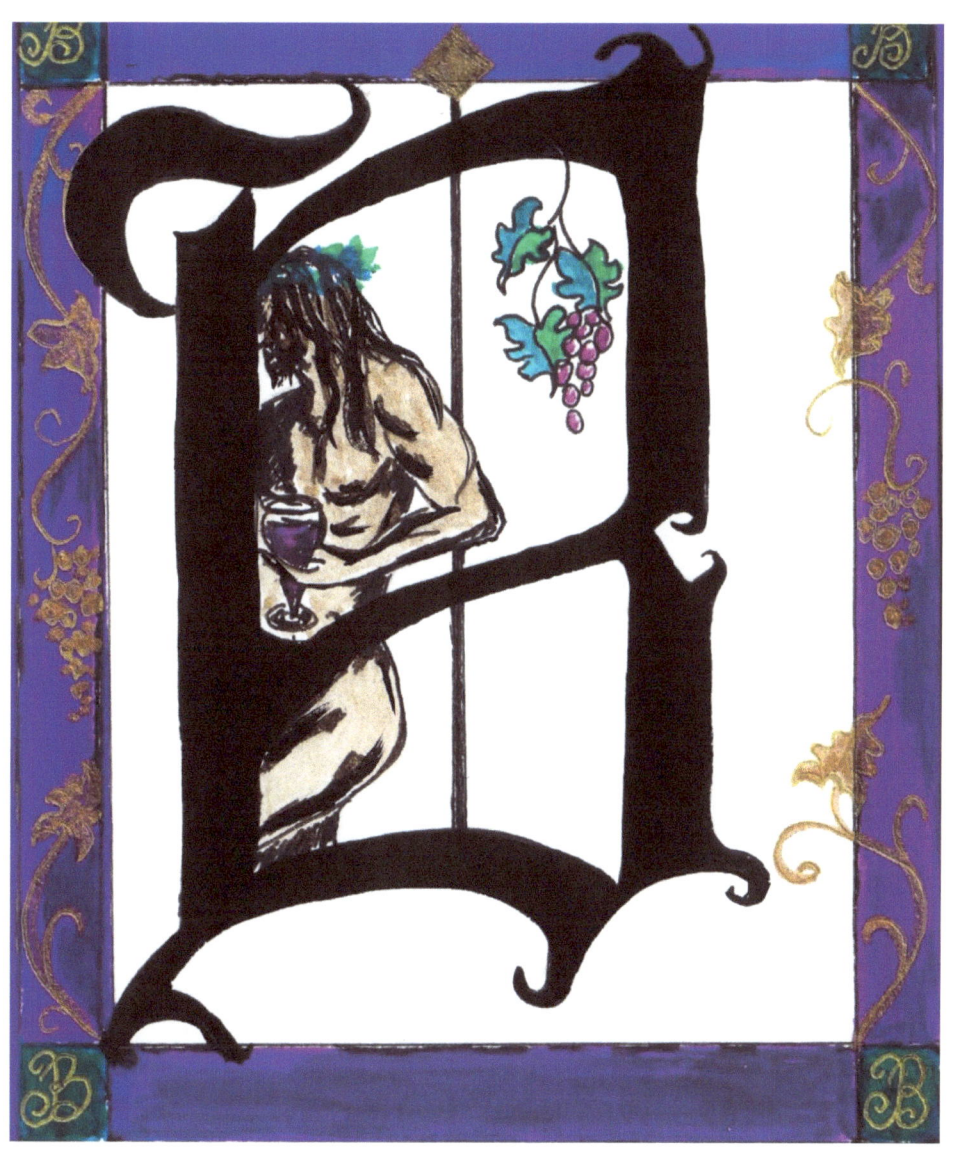

Fun and wine
with Frolic divine
come drink and dance
while you still
have a chance

Cat

To catch some raining stars

Gaze into a feline's

Shining eyes

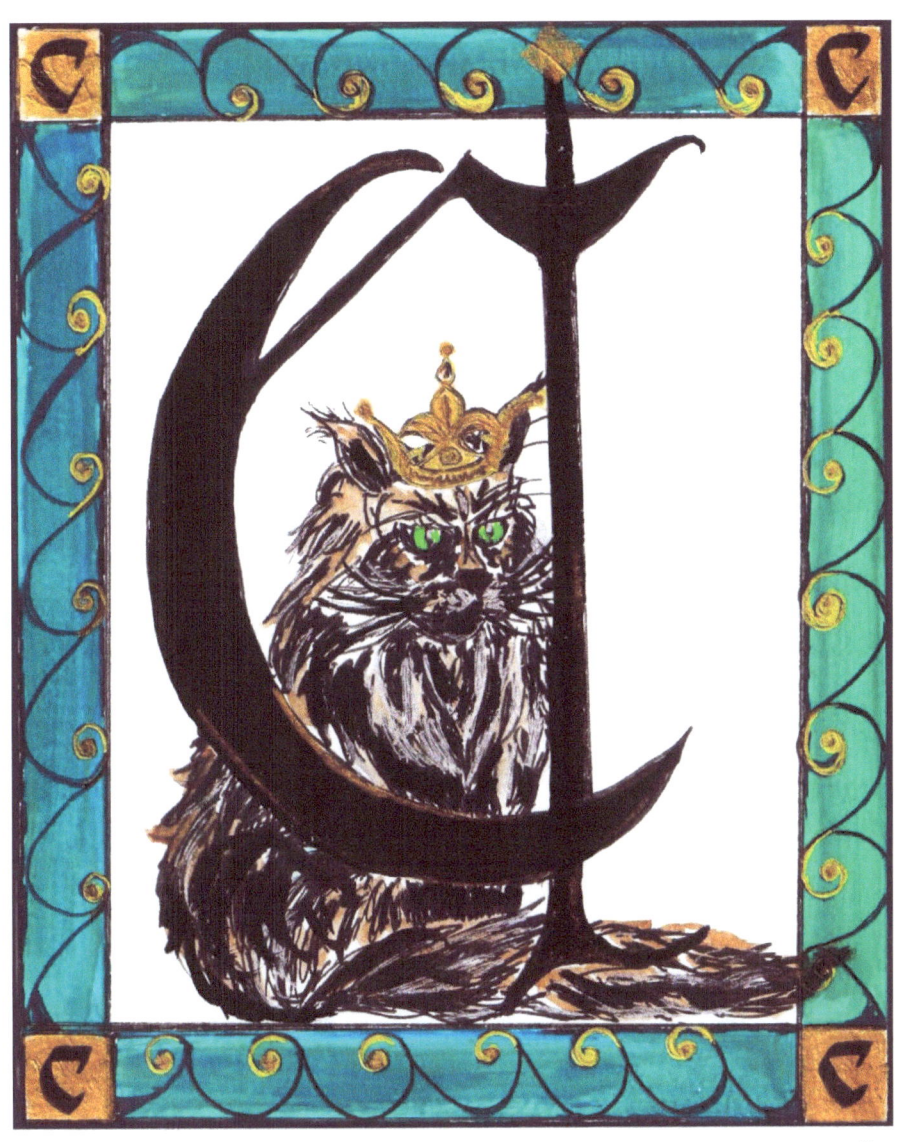

To catch some raining stars
Gaze into a feline's
Shining eyes

Dragon

The power, the beauty

The gold

Alluring tales of the old

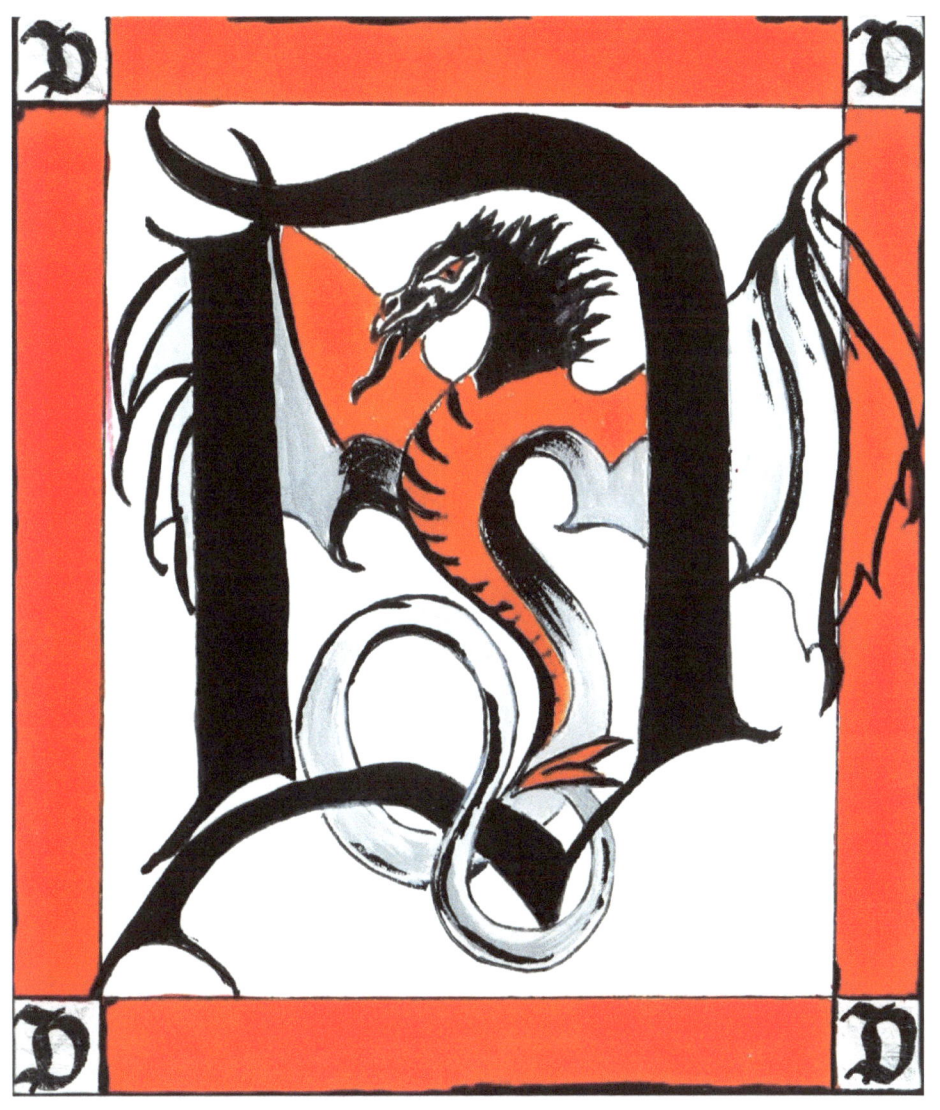

The power, the beauty
The gold
Alluring tales of the old

Elf

Over the land

And into the forest

Protector of fairy tales -

Warrior dear

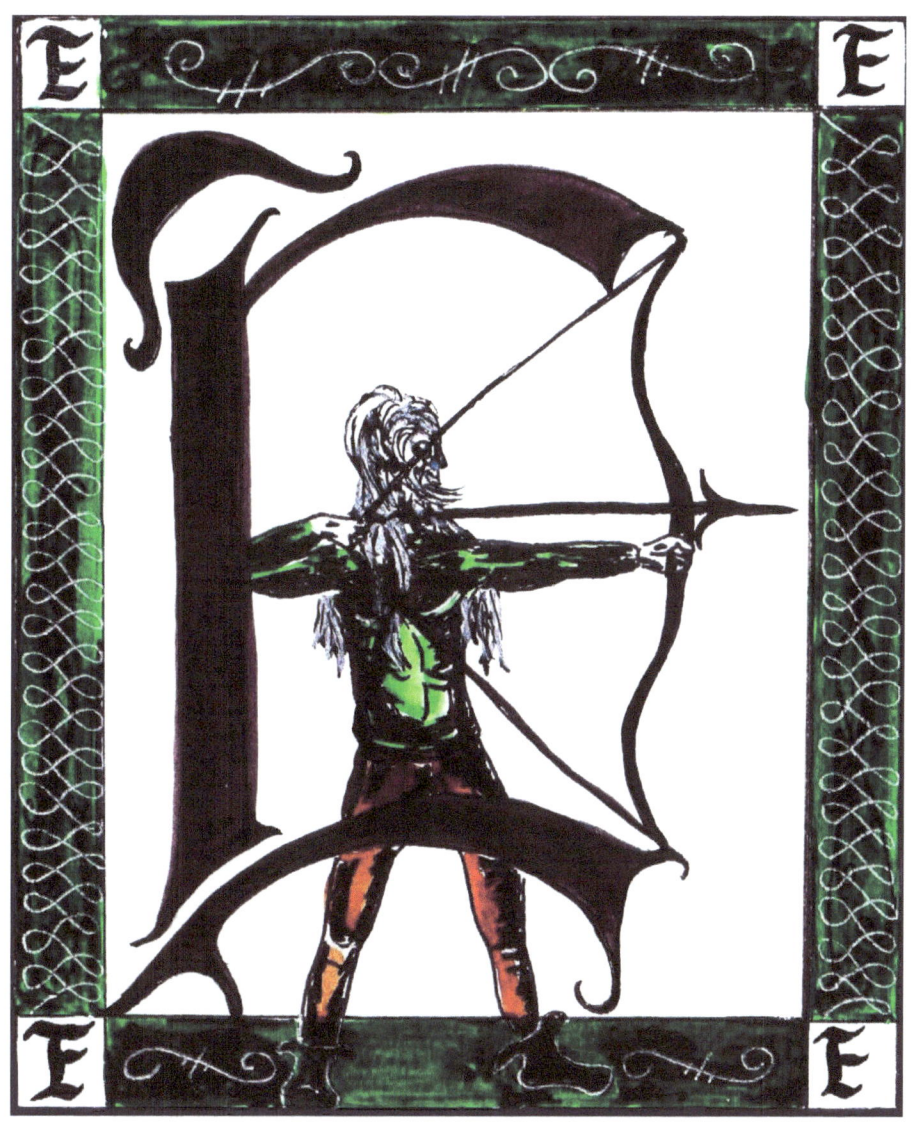

over the land
and into the forest
protector of
fairy tales ~
warrior dear

Faun

Ugly creature
Stellar heart
Kiss the frog
And trot afar

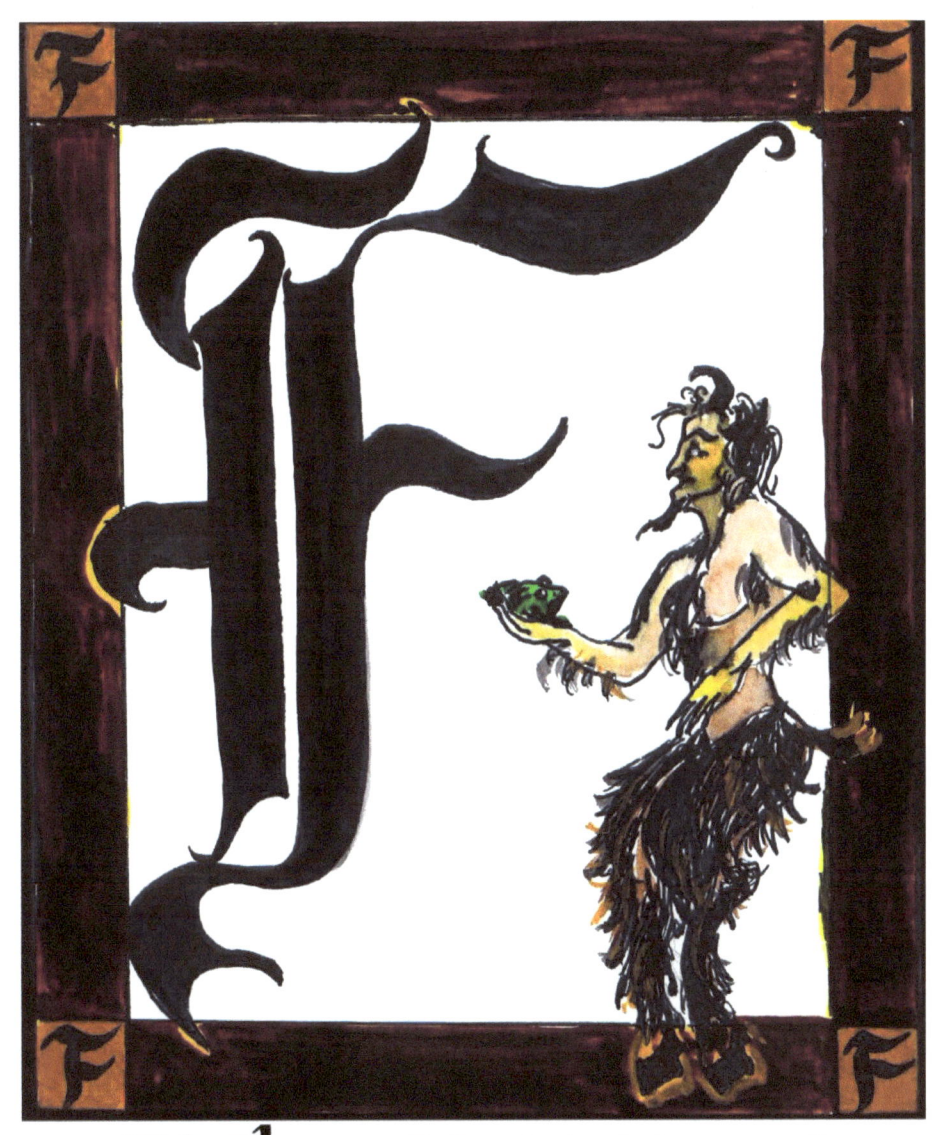

Ugly creature
stellar heart
kiss the frog
and trot afar

Gnome

Who dwells in the

Garden green?

The little folk in felt hats

And big grins

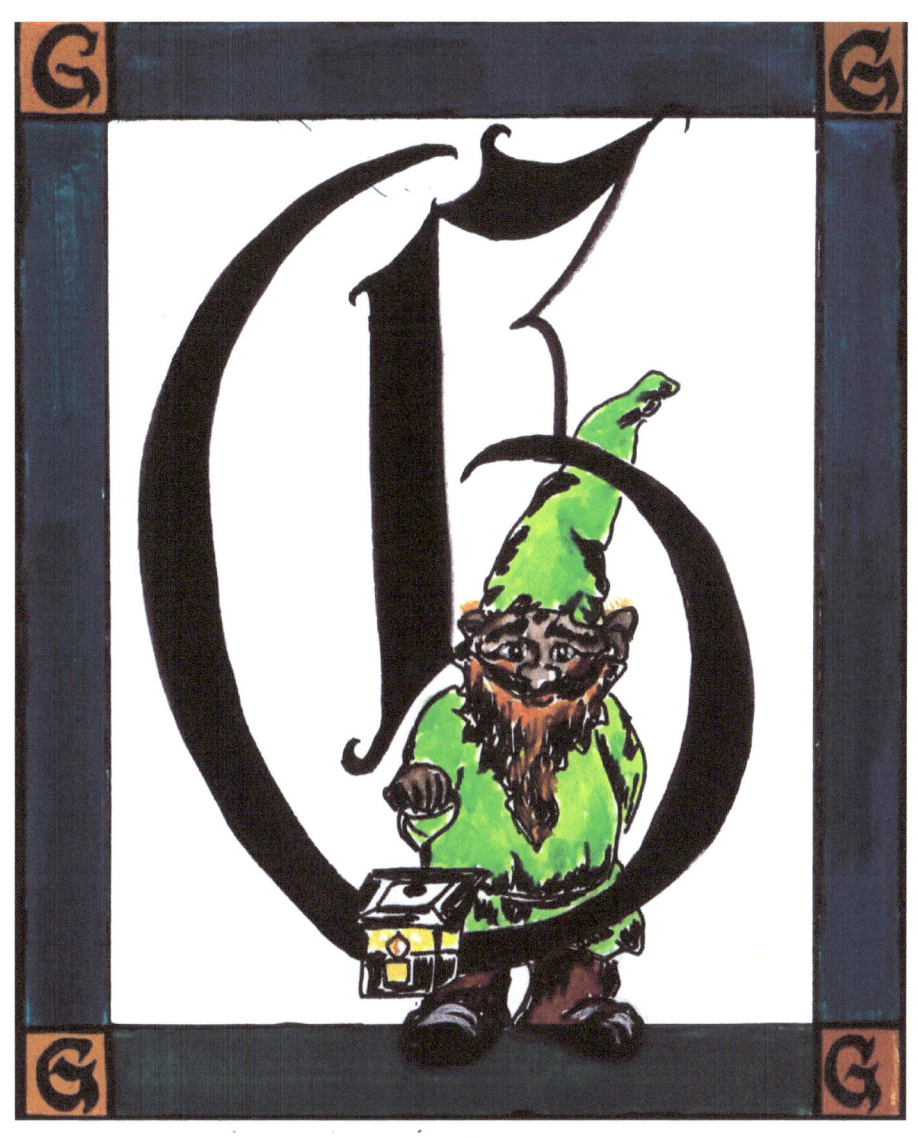

Who dwells in the
Garden green?
The little folk in felt hats
And big grins

Irish Harp

Magical sound

Of crystalline voice

Such tones come

By God's choice

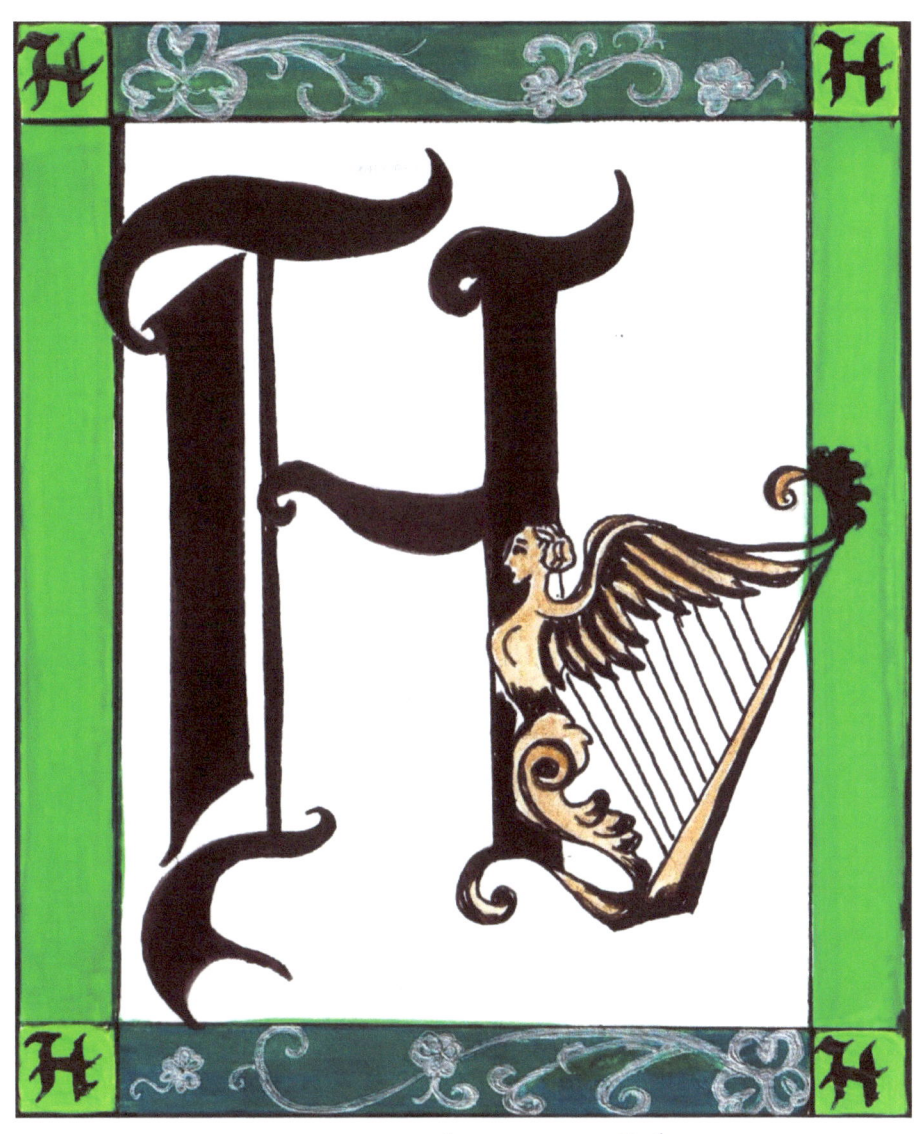

Magical sound
Of crystalline voice
Such tones come
By God's choice

Iris

Stately and tall
The bearded king
of flowers all

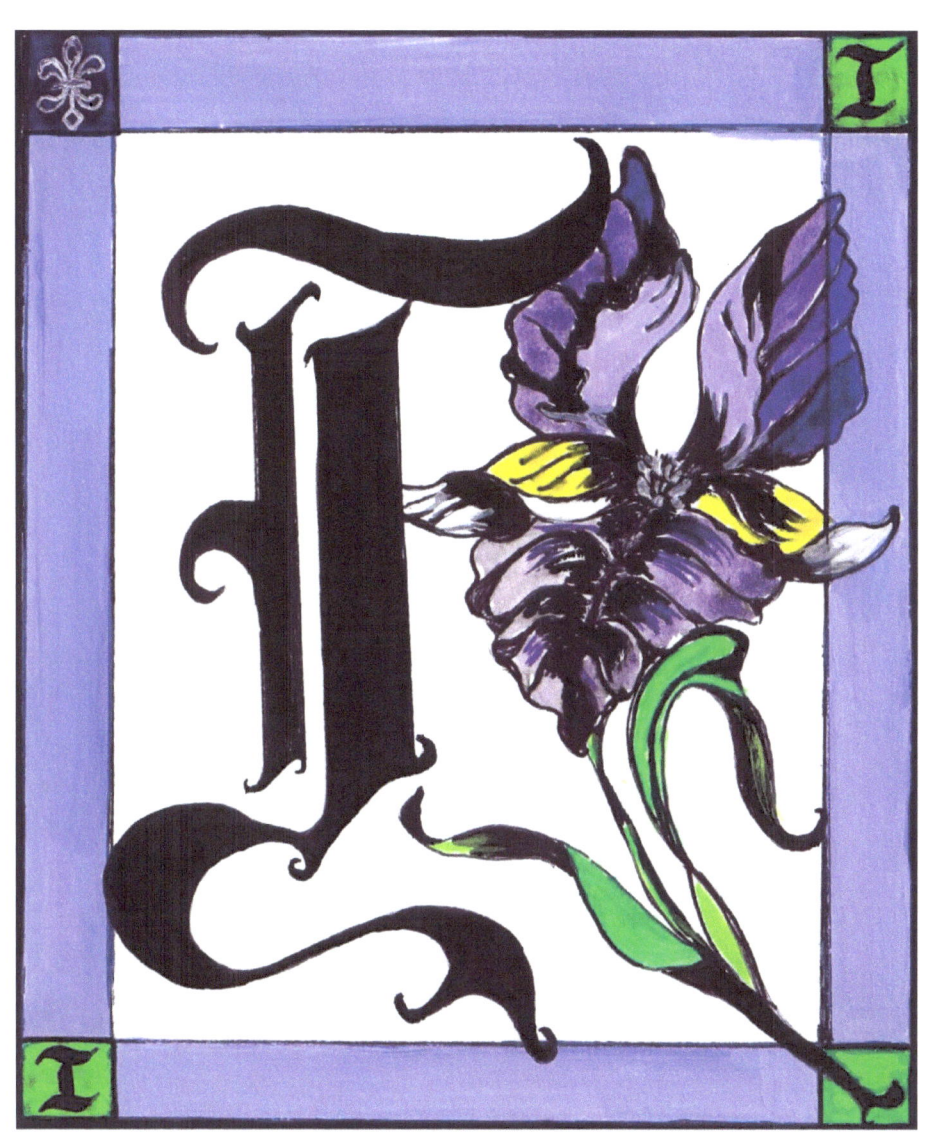

Stately and tall
The bearded king
Of flowers all

Jester

Poor Jester

Juggles many balls

For the reward

Of shiny cloth

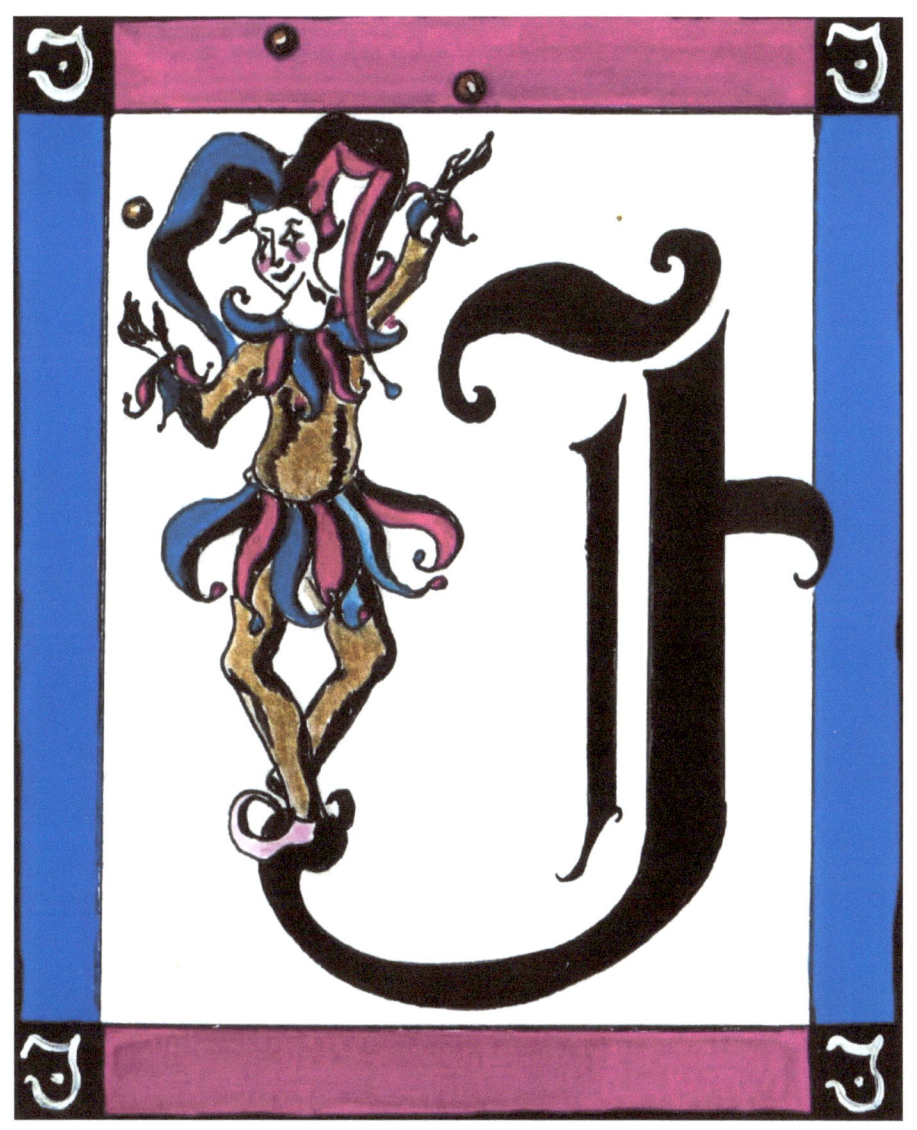

poor jester
juggles many balls
for the reward
of shiny cloth

Knight

The armour is heavy

The shield is strong

Faith and chivalry

Can't be wrong

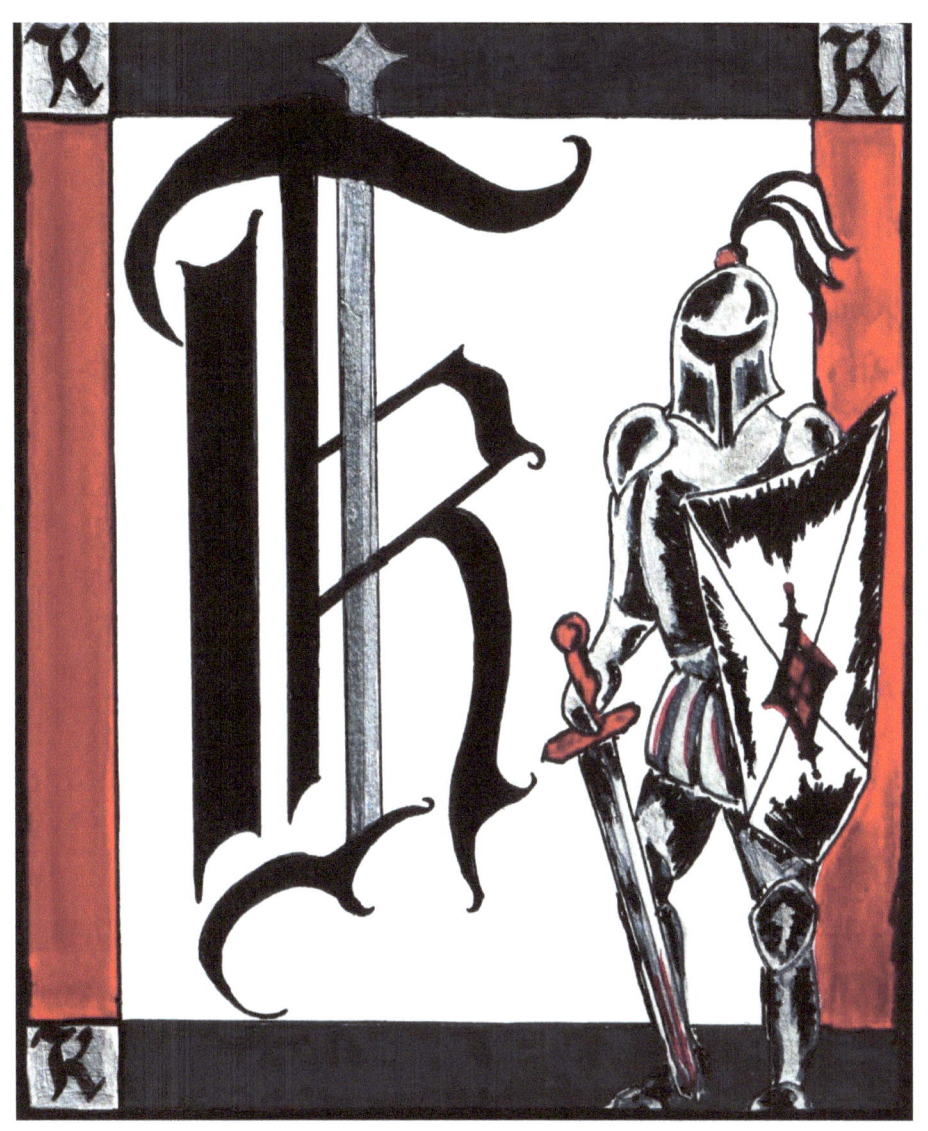

The armour is heavy
The shield is strong
Faith and chivalry
Can't be wrong

Luna

She comes by many names

To visit every clear night

But when we can't see her in the sky

Tis a case for fright

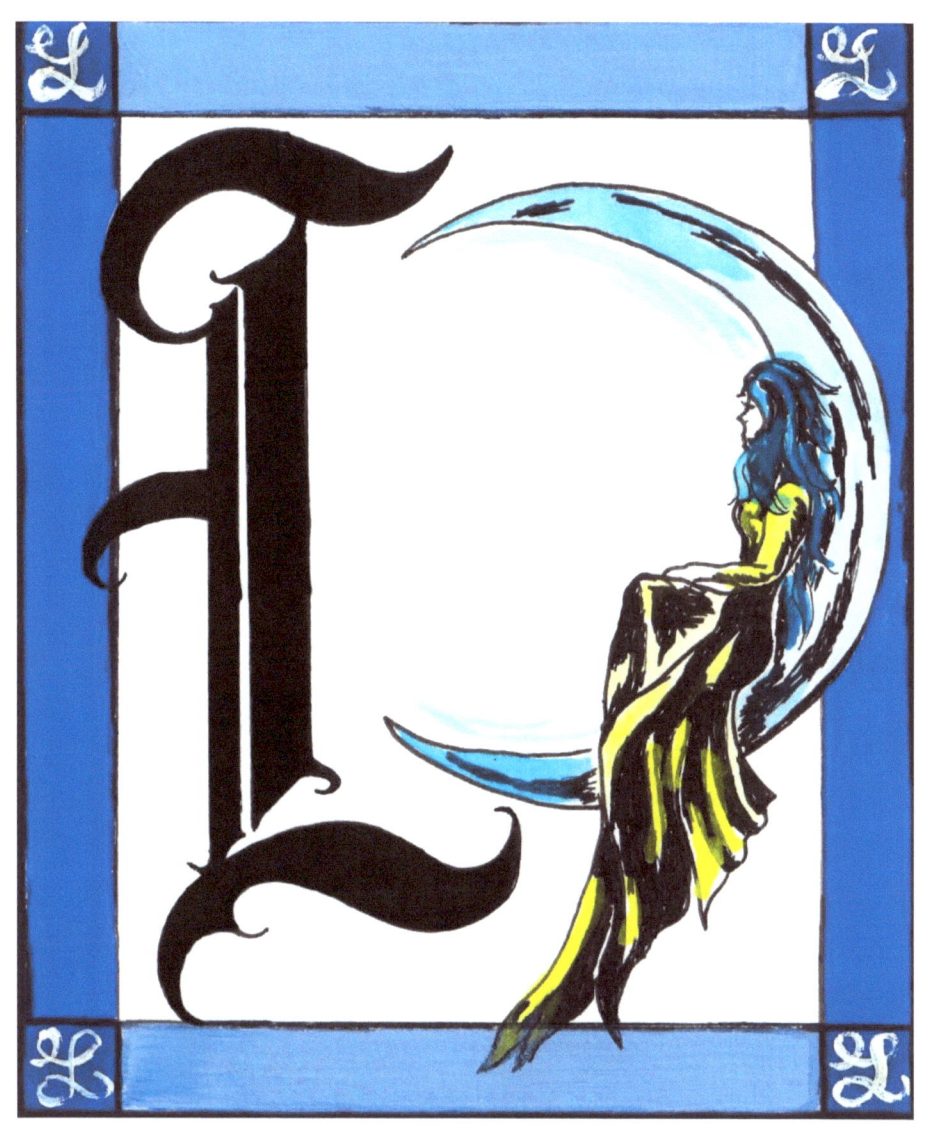

She comes by many names
To visit every clear night
But when we can't see her in the sky
'Tis a case for fright

Music

How to forget pain?

How to feel alive?

How to gain purpose?

Listen up and jive!

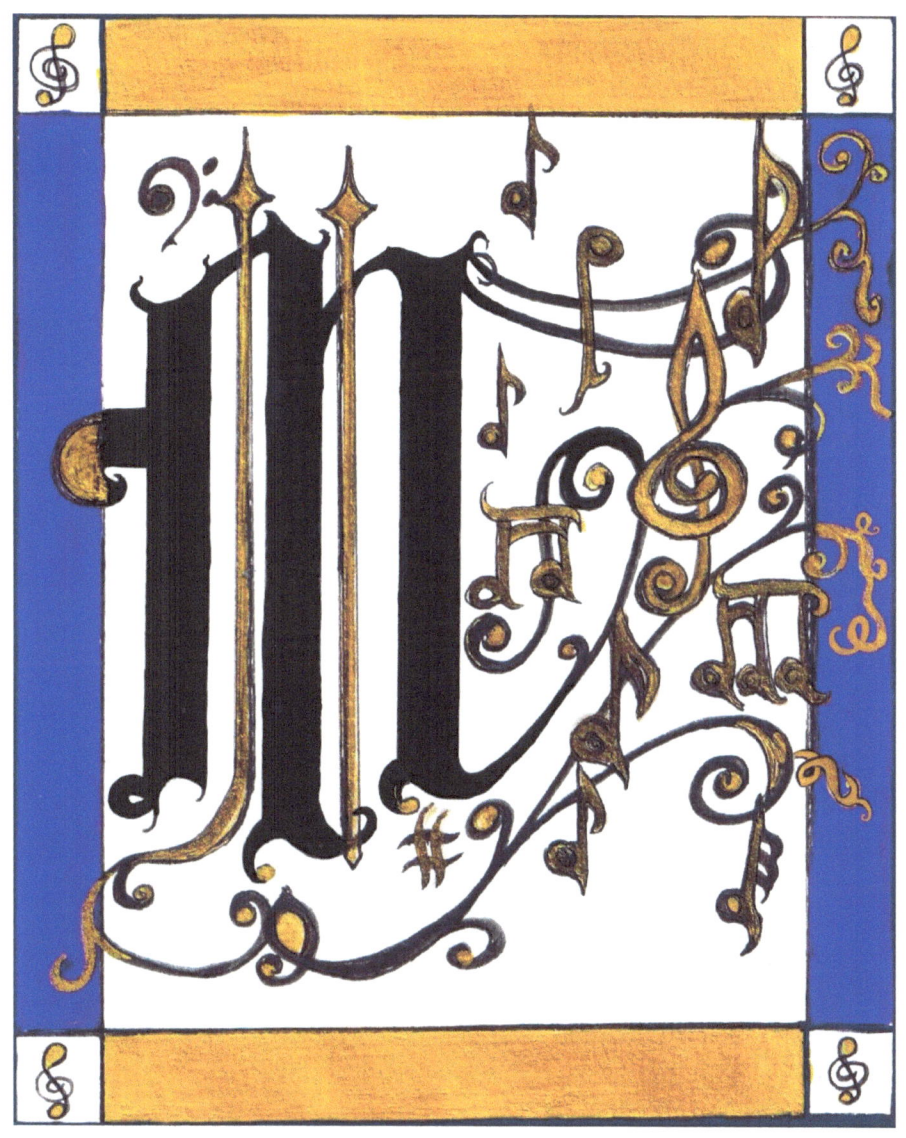

how to forget pain?
how to feel alive?
how to gain purpose?
listen up, and jive!

Nature

Beloved, cherished

Robbed, abused

Fight for her

Not to perish

And be overused

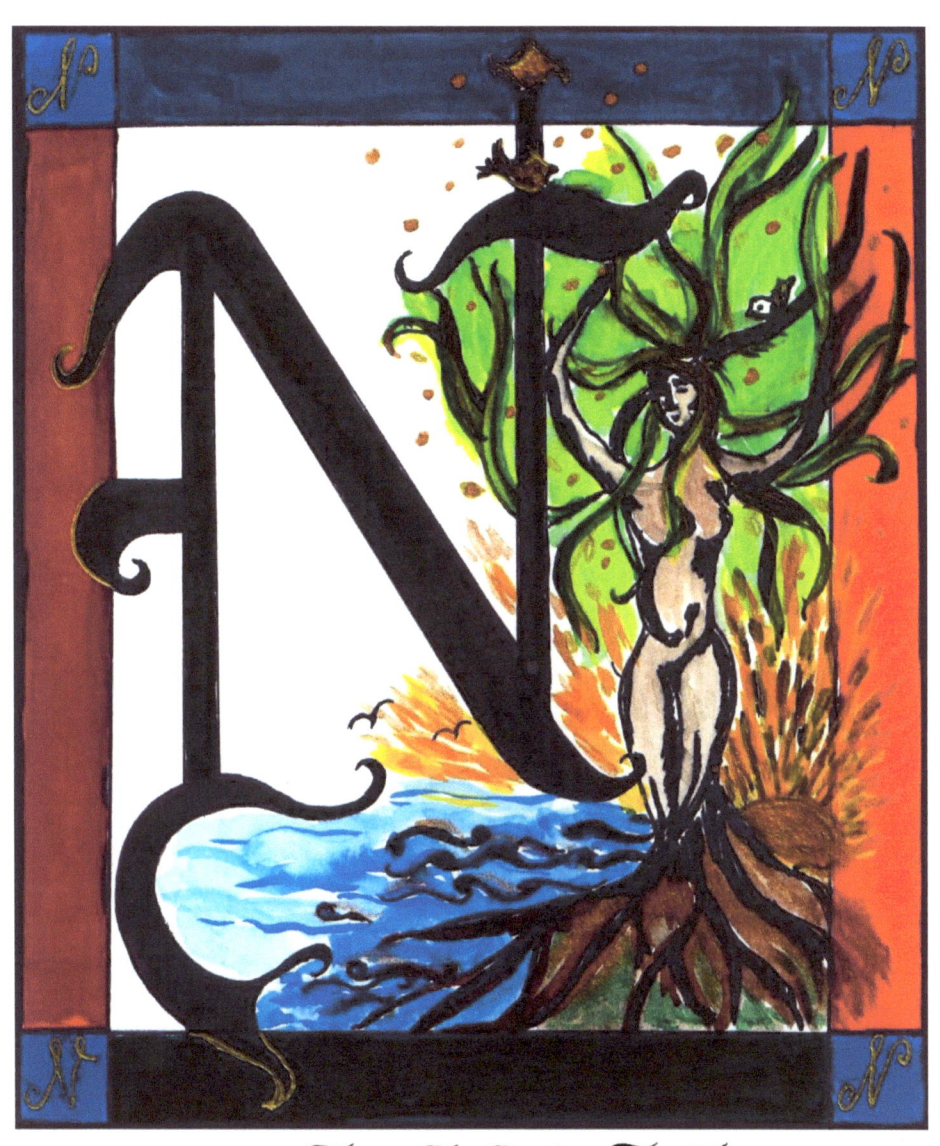

Beloved, cherished
Robbed, abused
Fight for her
Not to perish
And be overused

Owl

In barns and dark trees

By sharp talons and eyes

This creature protects us

Dear mice, say your

Goodbyes'

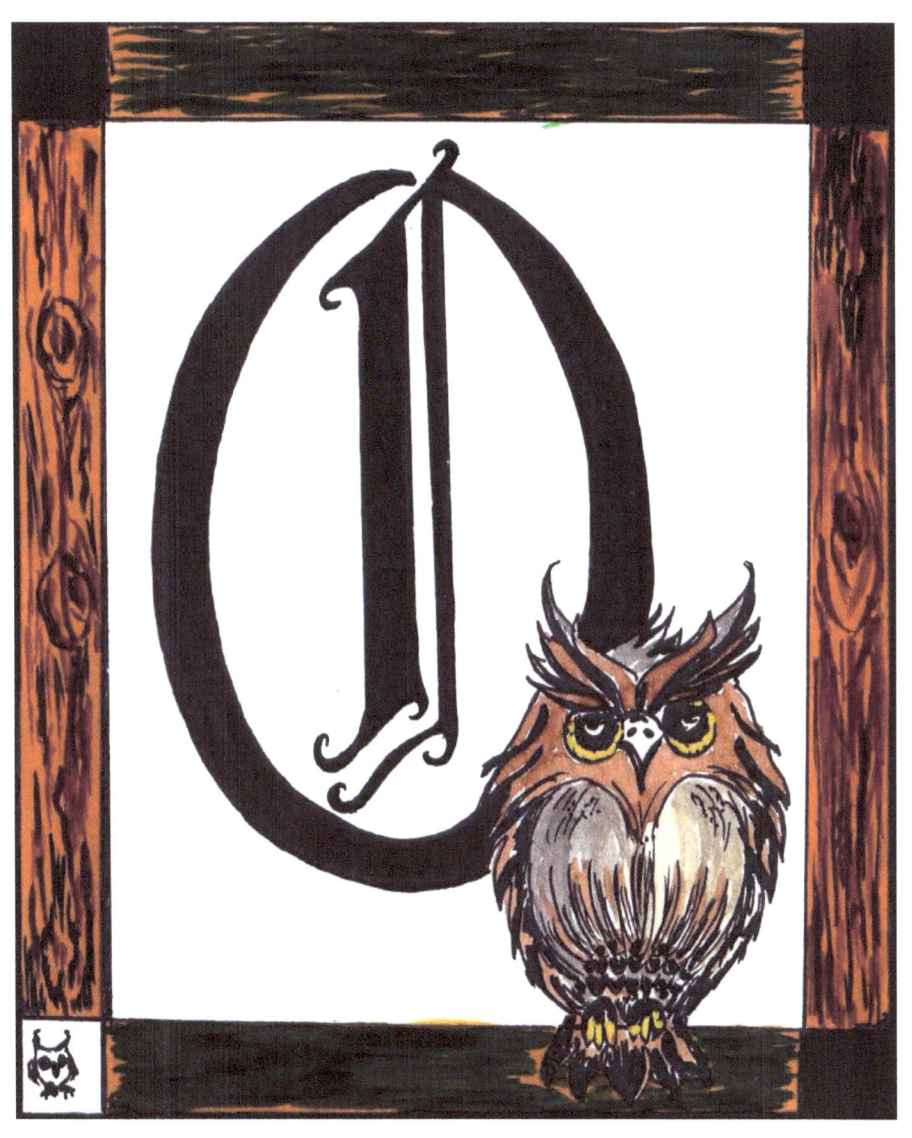

In barns and dark trees
By sharp talons and eyes
This creature protects us
Dear mice, say your
Goodbyes

Phoenix

Fiery bird born of its ashes

Beautiful wings

Can escape any jailer

Learn this lesson

And forget about failure

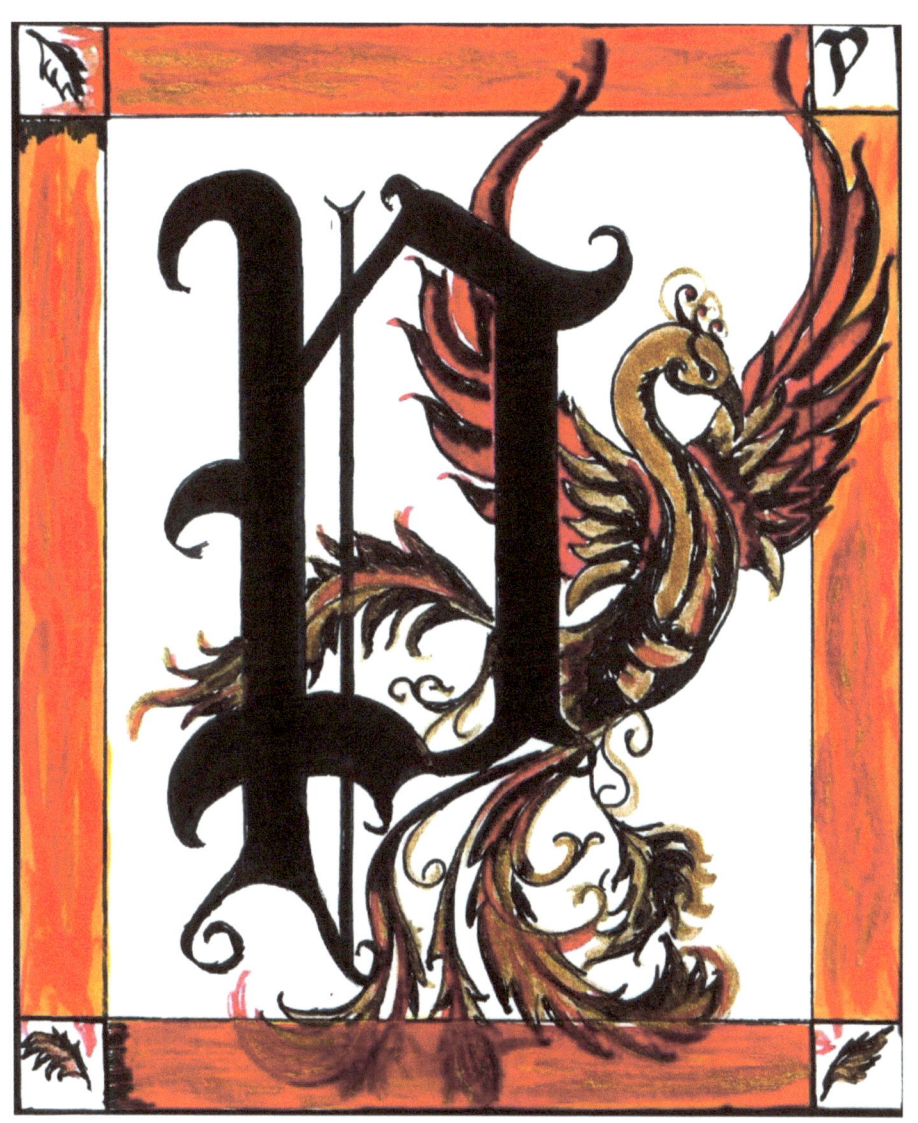

Fiery bird born of its ashes
Beautiful wings
Can escape any jailer
Learn this lesson
And forget about failure

Queen

Strict rules

Logical dame

A checkered past

Mrs. Chess is the name

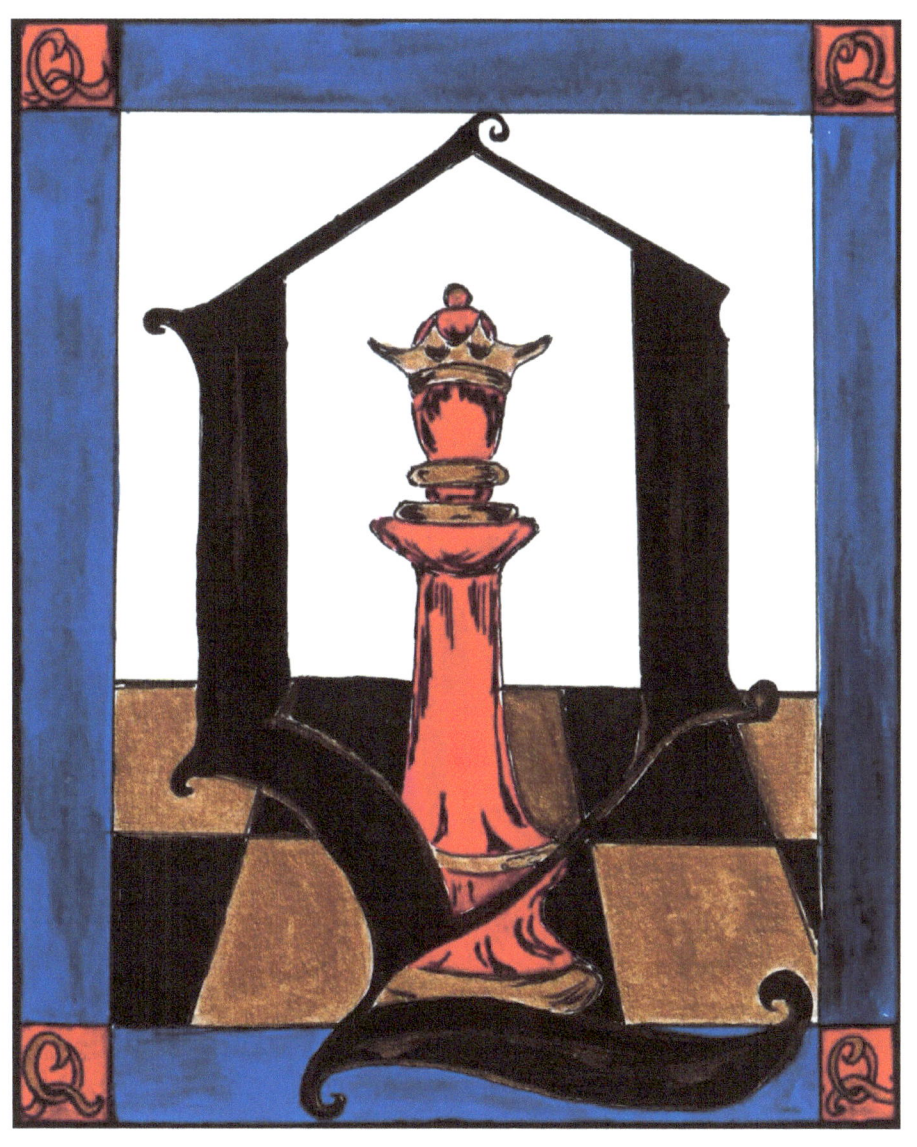

Strict rules
Logical dame
A checkered past
Mrs Chess — is the name

Raven

Who, who's knocking

On my door?

Mr. Poe had promised

This:

Nevermore

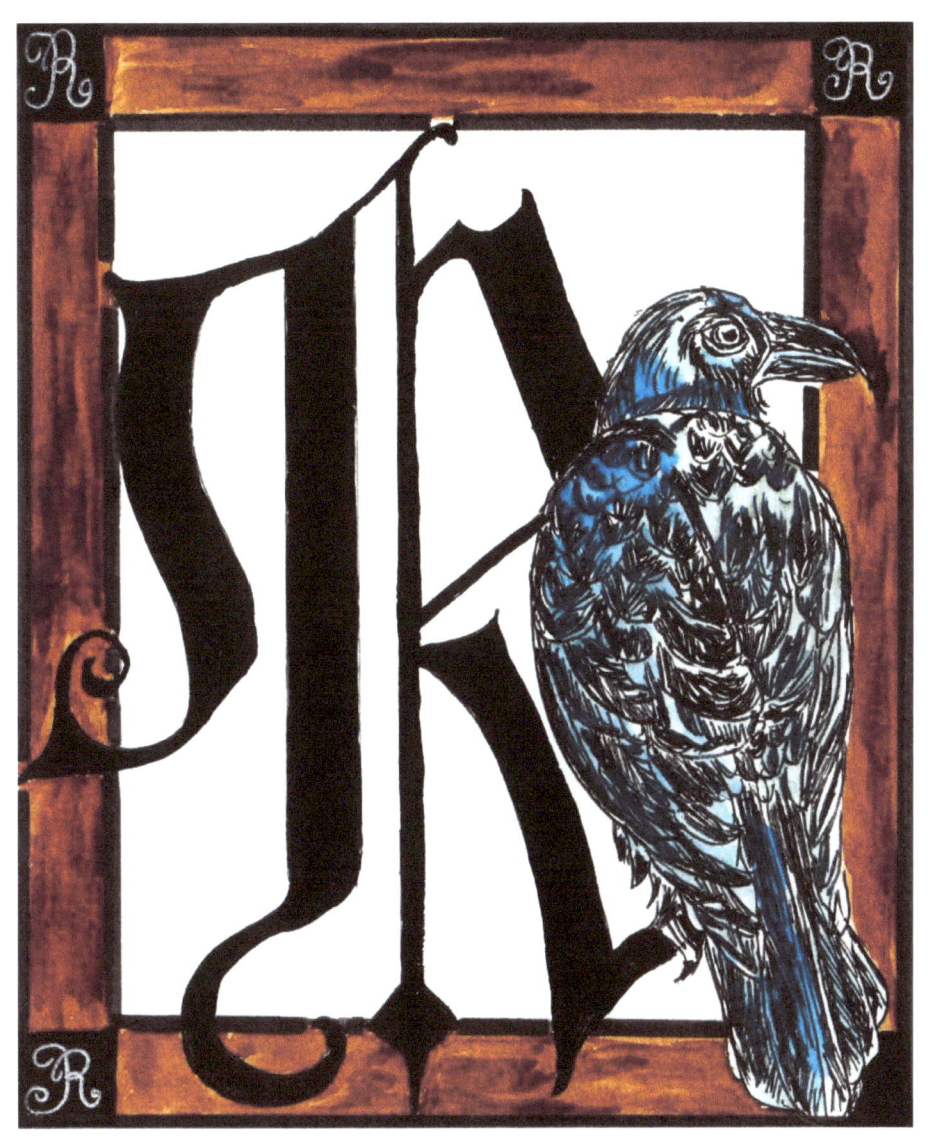

Who, who's knocking
On my door?
Mr. Poe had promised
This:
Nevermore

Skulls

Day of the Dead

We rejoice

Not dread

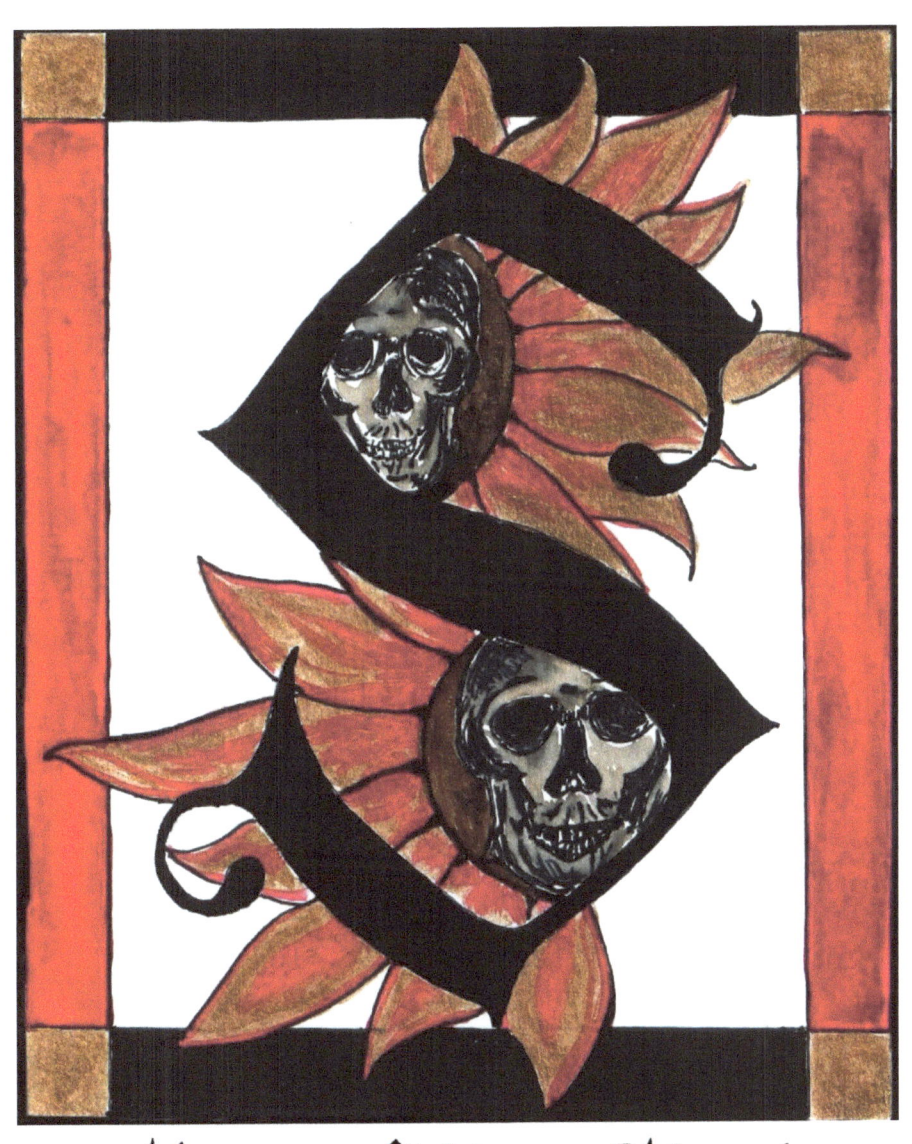

Time

Time is a train

Hurdling through space

We are the passengers

Watching the scenery go by

Fast without grace

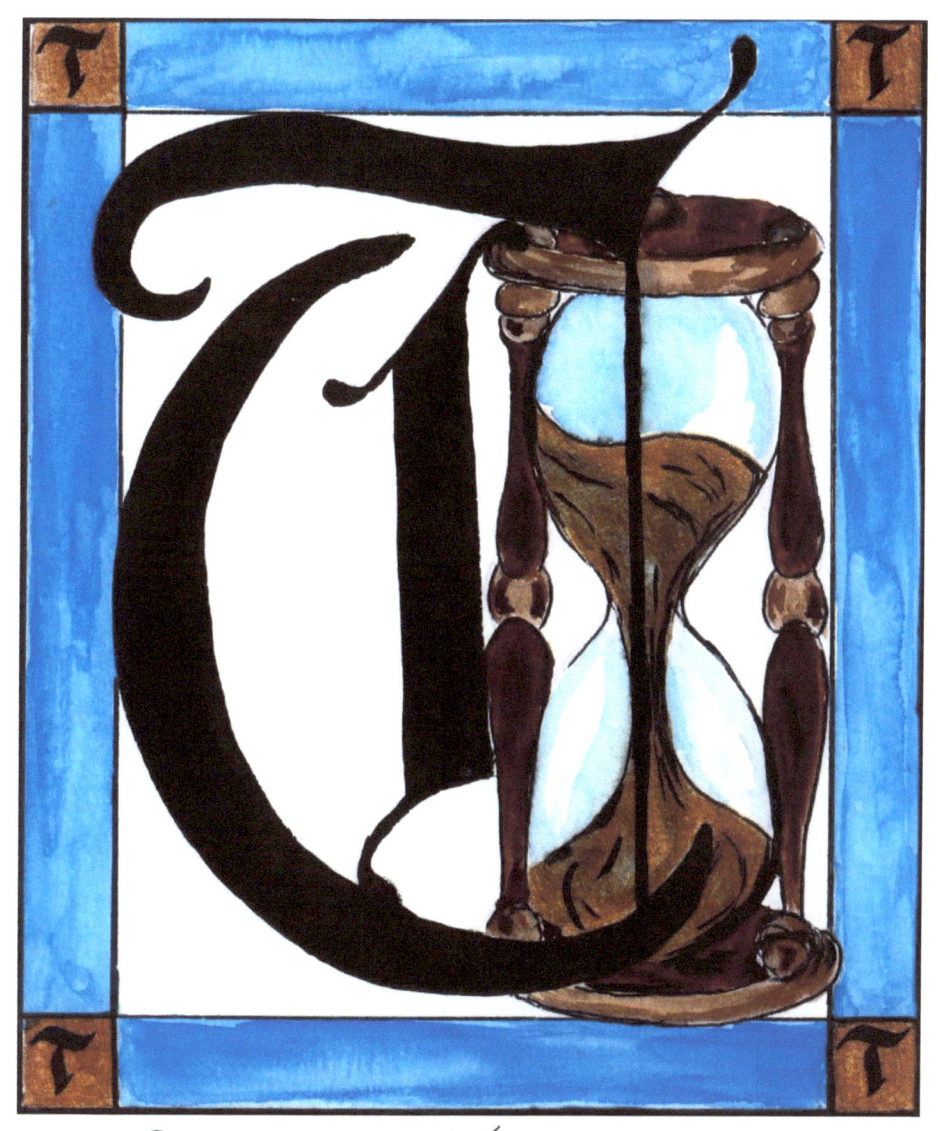

Time is a train
Hurdling through space
We are the passengers
Watching the scenery go by
Fast without grace

Unicorn

Silver beast on my mind

Beautiful eternal life

No such thing will I ever find

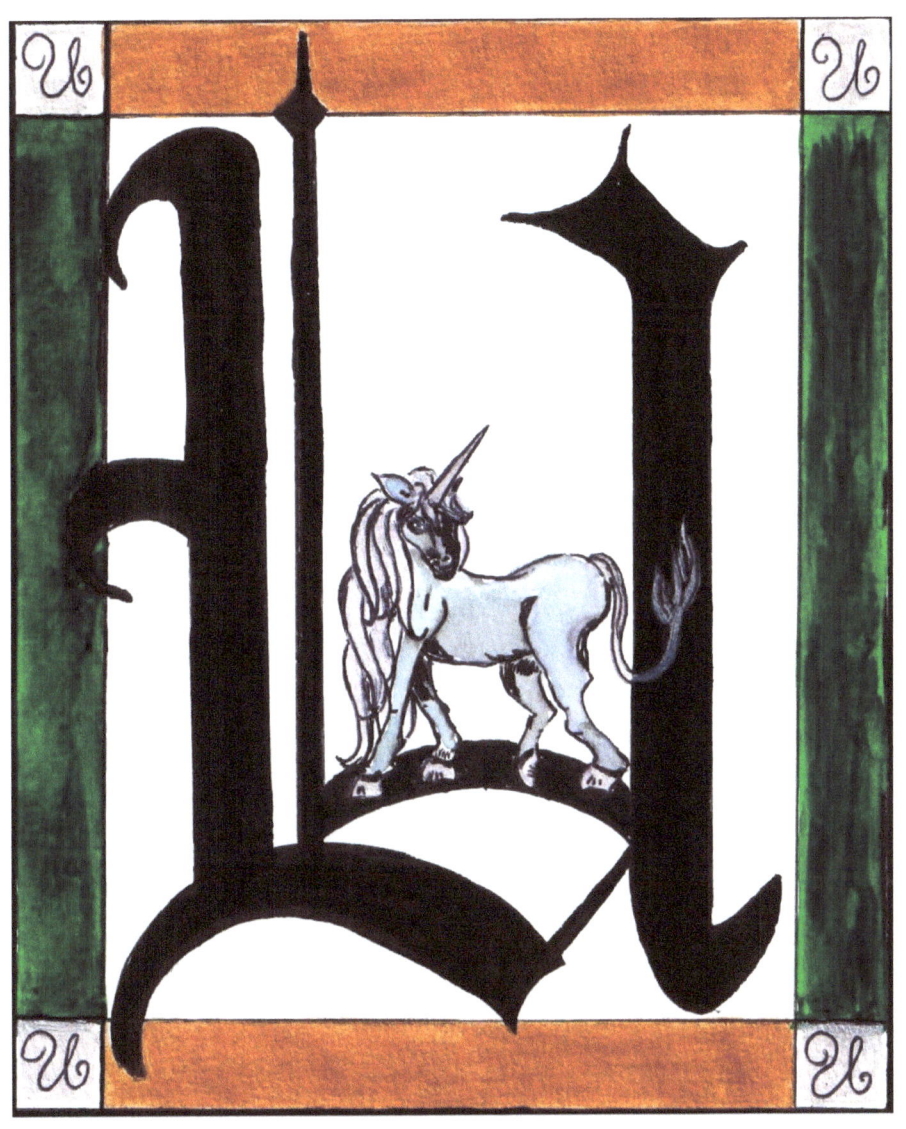

Silver beast on my mind
Beautiful eternal life
No such thing will I ever find

Vampire

Part comic, part sad

Novels about you

To read I am glad

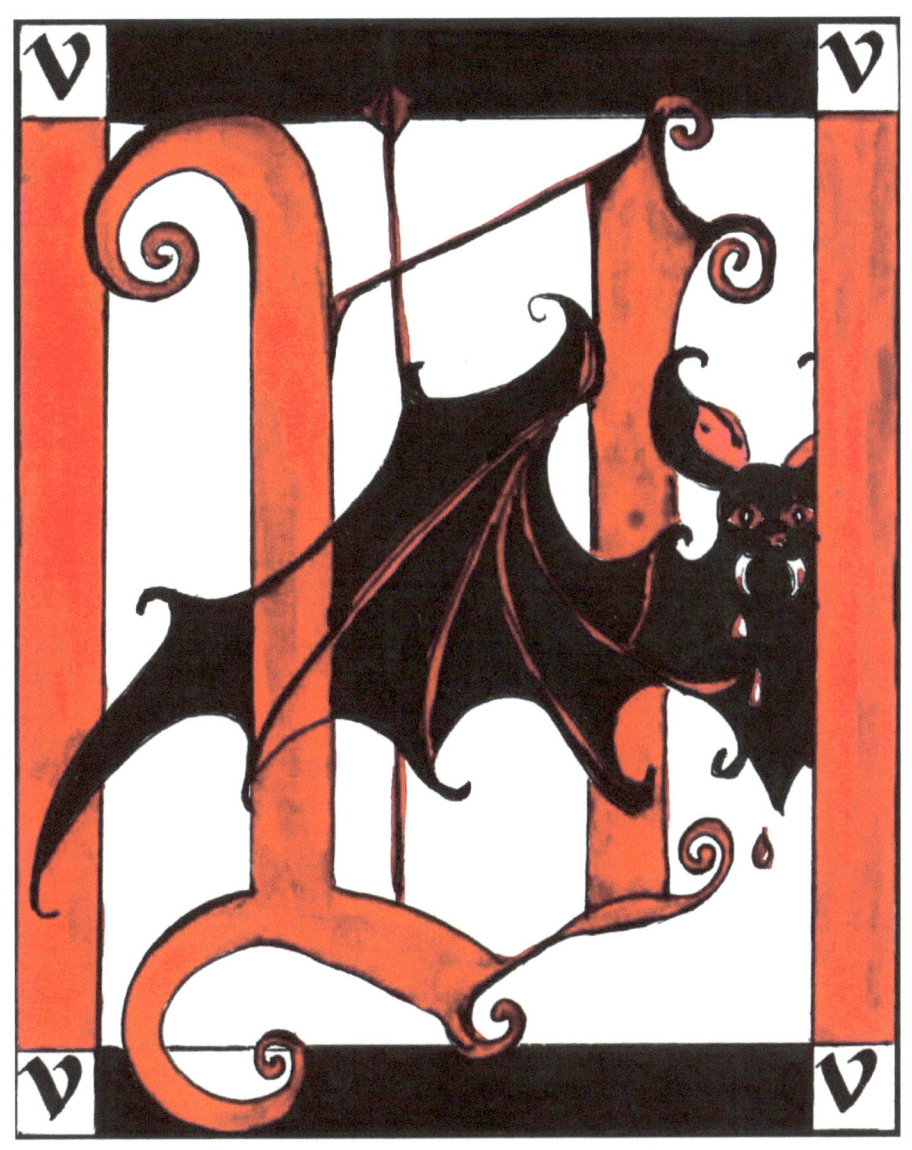

Part comic, part sad
Novels about you
To read I am glad

Witch

She bakes, she knits

She can fly on a broom

A most perfect friend

From here to the moon

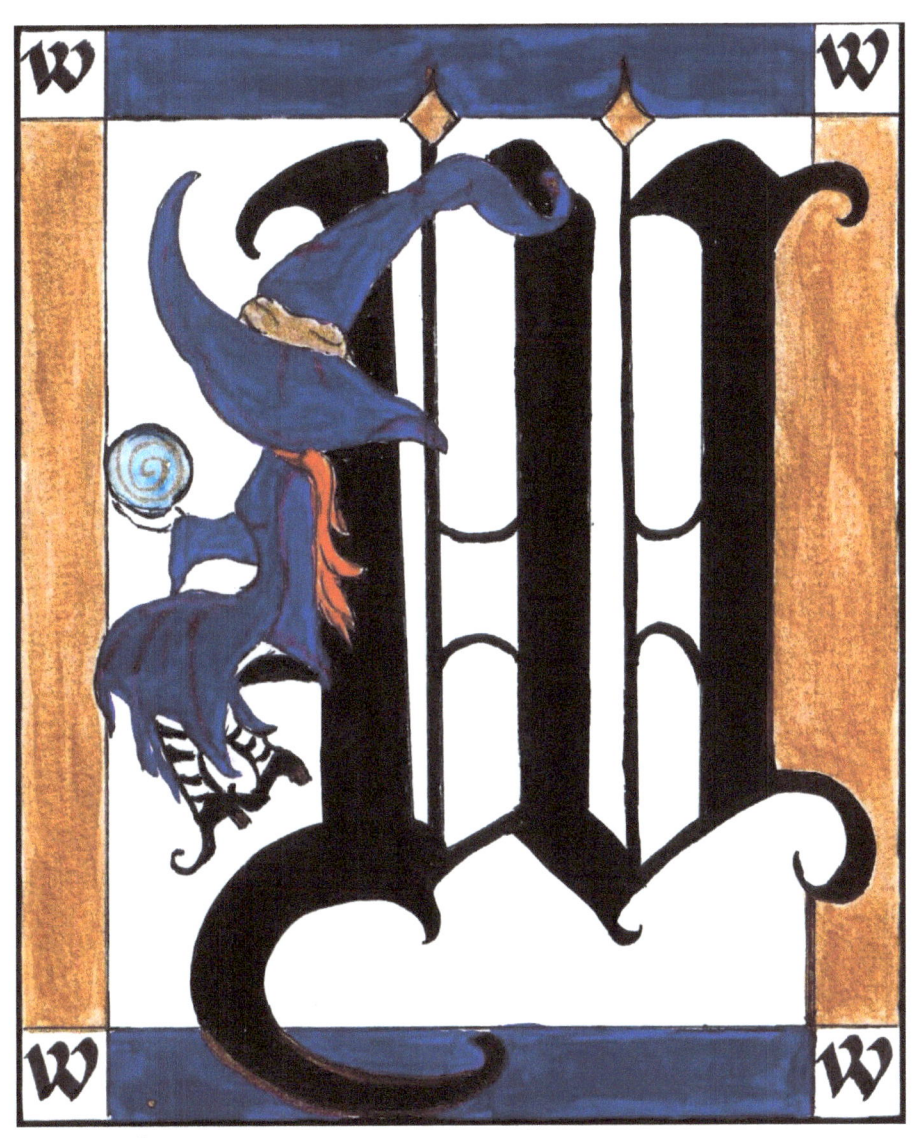

she bakes, she knits

she can fly on a broom

a most perfect friend

from here to the moon

Mr. X

Square jaw, steely eye
Who are you, mystery man,
Why leave
Without saying goodbye?

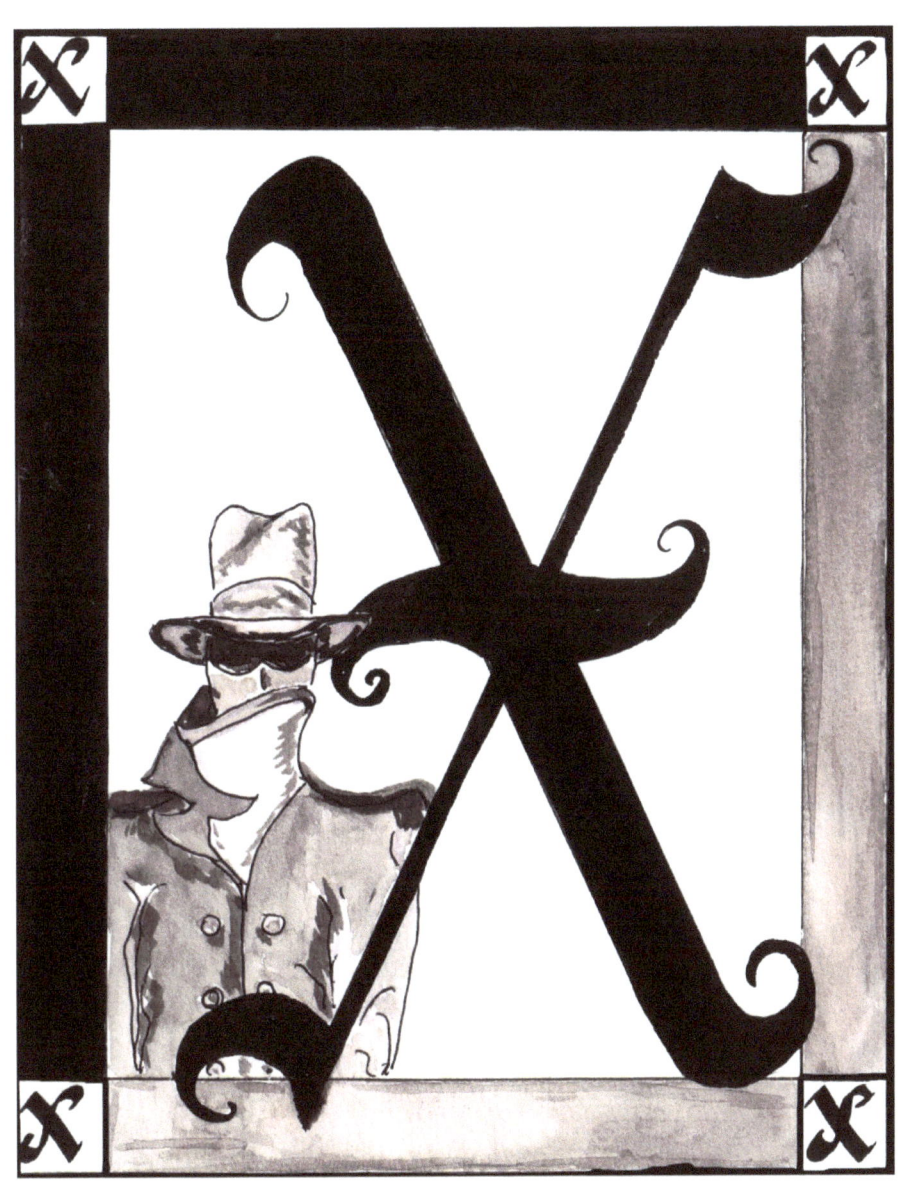

Square jaw, steely eye
Who are you, mystery man,
Why leave
Without saying goodbye?

Yoga

Be still, breathe, and pose

Like a porcelain figurine

Until serenity shows

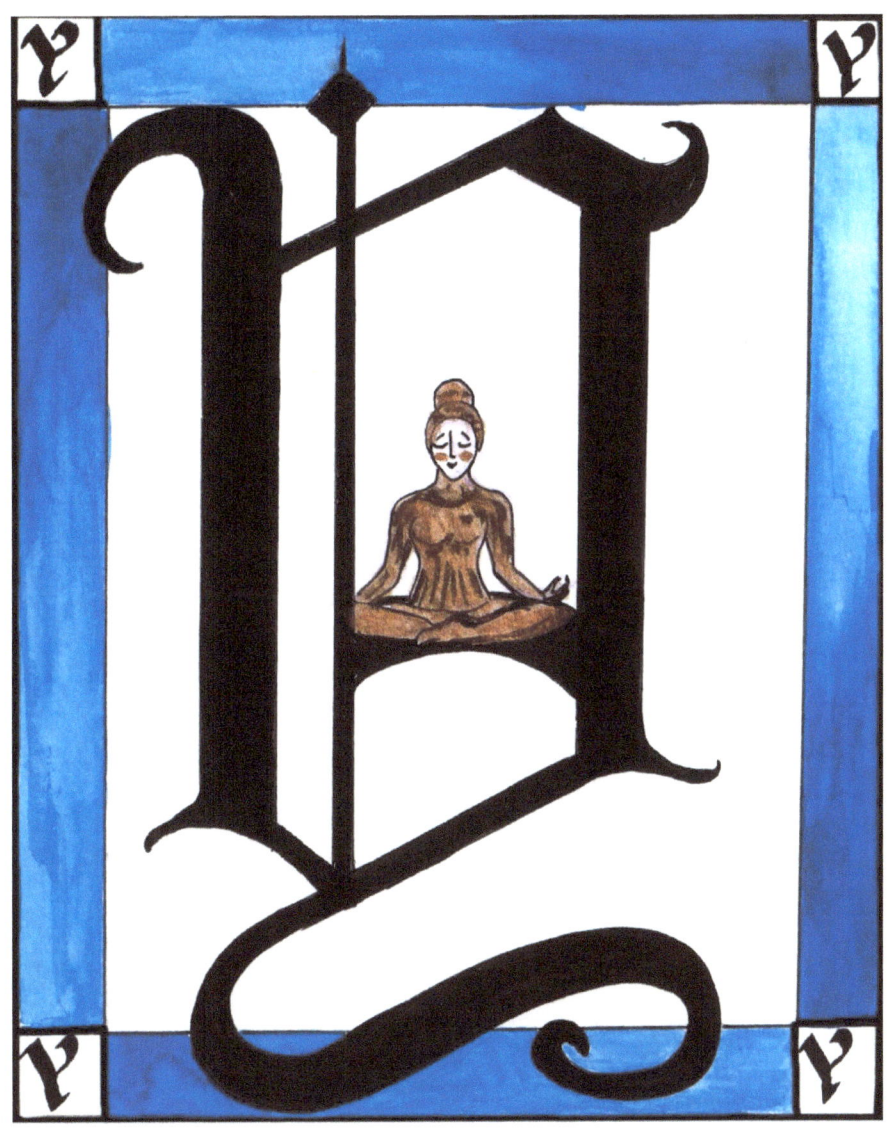

Be still, breathe, and pose
like a porcelain figurine
Until serenity shows

Zodiac

Fortune given by the stars

With multicoloured animals

And some with

Common elements

Foretell of our abilities

And love compatibilities

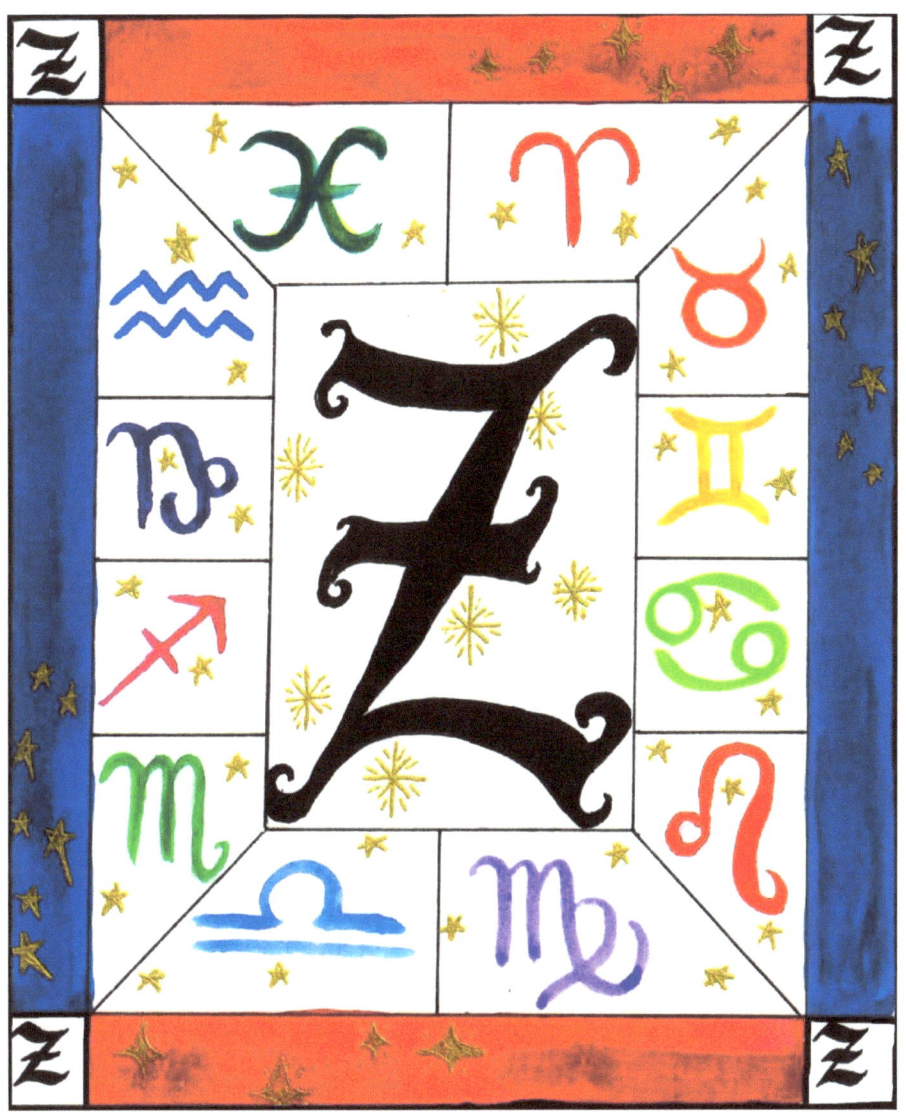

Fortune given by the stars
With multicoloured animals
And some with
Common elements
Foretell of our abilities
And love compatibilities

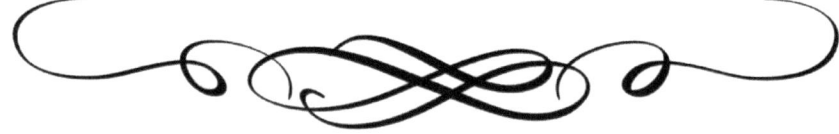

About The Author

Artist, teacher, and author Valerie Rachel Martin lives and creates in the beautiful Niagara Region, Ontario, Canada.

Inspired by nature and music she finds beauty in every corner of our round world. An avid traveler and story gatherer, she dedicates her life to art, and cherished four-legged companions.